Timeless Seeds of Advice

Allah

The Mighty and Magnificent

Al-Imam Ahmad

Ibn Taymiyyah: "...Indeed there is in the body a piece of flesh whish if it is sound then the whole body is sound, and if it is corrupt then the whole body is corrupt. Indeed it is the heart."

[Al-Bukhari, Muslim]

Great Books

Search by **ISBN** to buy the correct book

Stories of the Prophets	ISBN: 9781643543888
The Story of the Holy Prophet	ISBN: 9781643544267
The Noble Quran (Arabic)	ISBN: 9781643543994
Koran (English: Easy to Read)	ISBN: 9781643540924
Life in al-Barzakh: Life after Death	ISBN: 9781643544144
Disciplining the Soul	ISBN: 9781643544151
Timeless Seeds of Advice	ISBN: 9781643544120
Diseases of the Hearts & Cures	ISBN 9781643544106
The Path to Guidance	ISBN: 9781643544052
Miracles of the Prophet	ISBN: 9781643544038
Seerah of Prophet Muhammad	ISBN: 9781643543222
Book on Islam and Marriage	ISBN: 9781073877140
Great Women of Islam	ISBN: 9781643543758
Stories of the Koran	ISBN: 9781095900796
The Purification of the Soul	ISBN: 9781643541389
Al-Fawaid: Wise Sayings	ISBN: 9781727812718
The Book of Hajj	ISBN: 9781072243335
40 Hadith Qudsi	ISBN: 9781070655949
40 Hadith Nawawi	ISBN: 9781070547428
The Legacy of the Prophet	ISBN: 9781080249343
The Ideal Muslim Woman	ISBN: 9781643543192
The Soul's Journey after Death	ISBN: 9781643541365
Khalid Bin Al-Waleed	ISBN: 9781643543420
The Islamic View of Jesus	ISBN: 978164354335
Don't Be Sad	ISBN: 9781643543451
Ota Benga	ISBN: 9798698096665

Chapter 1: The Jannah

Deeds are never sufficient to deliver a person from the Fire, or to grant a person entry into the Jannah (Paradise). This can only come about through the mercy of Allah the Almighty. The Quran supports this view in many places such as His sayings:

بِسْمِ اللَّهِ الرَّحْمَٰنِ الرَّحِيمِ ﴿١﴾

In the name of Allah, the Entirely Merciful, the Especially Merciful.

إِنَّ الَّذِينَ ءَامَنُوا۟ وَالَّذِينَ هَاجَرُوا۟ وَجَٰهَدُوا۟ فِى سَبِيلِ اللَّهِ أُو۟لَٰٓئِكَ يَرْجُونَ رَحْمَتَ اللَّهِ ۚ وَاللَّهُ غَفُورٌ رَّحِيمٌ ﴿٢١٨﴾

Indeed, those who have believed and those who have emigrated and fought in the cause of Allah - those expect the mercy of Allah. And Allah is Forgiving and Merciful. [2:218]

يُبَشِّرُهُمْ رَبُّهُم بِرَحْمَةٍ مِّنْهُ وَرِضْوَٰنٍ وَجَنَّٰتٍ لَّهُمْ فِيهَا نَعِيمٌ مُّقِيمٌ ﴿٢١﴾

Their Lord gives them good tidings of mercy from Him and approval and of gardens for them wherein is enduring pleasure. [9:21]

بُؤْمِنُونَ بِاللَّهِ وَرَسُولِهِ وَتُجَاهِدُونَ فِي سَبِيلِ اللَّهِ بِأَمْوَالِكُمْ وَأَنفُسِكُمْ ذَلِكُمْ خَيْرٌ لَّكُمْ إِن كُنتُمْ تَعْلَمُونَ ﴿١١﴾

يَغْفِرْ لَكُمْ ذُنُوبَكُمْ وَيُدْخِلْكُمْ جَنَّاتٍ تَجْرِي مِن تَحْتِهَا الْأَنْهَارُ وَمَسَاكِنَ طَيِّبَةً فِي جَنَّاتِ عَدْنٍ ذَلِكَ الْفَوْزُ الْعَظِيمُ ﴿١٢﴾

It is to believe in Allah and His Messenger (peace be upon him) and strive in the cause of Allah with your wealth and your lives. That is best for you, if you should know. He will forgive for you your sins and admit you to gardens beneath which rivers flow and pleasant dwellings in gardens of perpetual residence. That is the great success. [61:11-12]

On the Day of Judgment, everyone will have either the forgiveness of Allah or the great Fire. And life is either a source of Allah's protection or a source of destruction.

On his death bed, Mohammad Ibn Wassy said goodbye to all his family and companions and said: "Peace be upon you, either to the Fire or to the Jannah through the mercy of Allah the Almighty." [Al-Hilyah]

As for the saying of Allah:

وَتِلْكَ الْجَنَّةُ الَّتِىٓ أُورِثْتُمُوهَا بِمَا كُنتُمْ تَعْمَلُونَ ۝

لَكُمْ فِيهَا فَٰكِهَةٌ كَثِيرَةٌ مِّنْهَا تَأْكُلُونَ ۝

And that is Jannah which you are made to inherit for what you used to do in life. For you therein is much fruit from which you will eat. [43:72-73]

Islamic scholars differed about the meaning of this, falling into different opinions: Entry into Jannah is accorded by Allah's mercy, however the assignment of ranking and the station in Jannah is done in accordance to the deeds one done in their life.

Ibn Uyaynah said: "They were of the opinion that salvation from the Fire occurs through the mercy and forgiveness of Allah alone, and entry into Jannah occurs by His grace alone, but the apportioning of ranking occurs in accordance to one's deeds."

Al-Hasan Al-Basri, may Allah have mercy on him, said: "Indeed, those who came before you saw the Quran as personal letters from Allah the Almighty. So they pondered over it by night and yearned for it by day."

كُلُوا۟ وَٱشْرَبُوا۟ هَنِيٓـَٔۢا بِمَا كُنتُمْ تَعْمَلُونَ ﴿١٩﴾

They will be told: "Eat and drink in satisfaction for what you used to do." [52:19]

أَمَّا ٱلَّذِينَ ءَامَنُوا۟ وَعَمِلُوا۟ ٱلصَّـٰلِحَـٰتِ فَلَهُمْ جَنَّـٰتُ ٱلْمَأْوَىٰ نُزُلًۢا بِمَا كَانُوا۟ يَعْمَلُونَ ﴿١٩﴾

As for those who believe (in the Oneness of Allah Islamic Monotheism) and do righteous good deeds, for them are Gardens (Paradise) as an entertainment, for what they used to do. [32:19]

No one will enter into Jannah by virtue of the deeds alone. The actual entry into Jannah is always dependent upon the grace of Allah alone, His Forgiveness and Mercy. Allah is the one who blessed humans with the means and the result of that means. Hence entry is not a direct outcome of actions in and of themselves.

Prophet Muhammad, peace and blessings be upon him, said: "Allah, the Blessed and the Exalted, said to Jannah: You are My Mercy, I show mercy through you to whoever I will of My servants."

إِنَّ ٱلَّذِينَ قَالُوا۟ رَبُّنَا ٱللَّهُ ثُمَّ ٱسْتَقَمُوا۟ تَتَنَزَّلُ عَلَيْهِمُ ٱلْمَلَـٰٓئِكَةُ أَلَّا تَخَافُوا۟ وَلَا تَحْزَنُوا۟ وَأَبْشِرُوا۟ بِٱلْجَنَّةِ ٱلَّتِى كُنتُمْ تُوعَدُونَ ﴿٣٠﴾

Indeed, those who have said: "Our Lord is Allah, and then Istaqamu (remained on a right course) - the angels will descend upon them, [saying], "Do not fear and do not grieve but receive good tidings of Paradise, which you were promised." [41:30]

The servants have no right over Allah that He must render. Never! Neither, in His presence, is any effort wretched. If man is punished, then by His Justice, and if man is in bliss, then by His beneficence. He is the King, the Kind, the Vast, and the Merciful.

Ibn al-Qayyim, may Allah have mercy on him, said: "Never belittle a small sin, for the biggest of fires can be caused by the smallest sparks."

9

يَٰبُنَىَّ إِنَّهَآ إِن تَكُ مِثْقَالَ حَبَّةٍ مِّنْ خَرْدَلٍ فَتَكُن فِى صَخْرَةٍ أَوْ فِى ٱلسَّمَٰوَٰتِ أَوْ فِى ٱلْأَرْضِ يَأْتِ بِهَا ٱللَّهُ إِنَّ ٱللَّهَ لَطِيفٌ خَبِيرٌ ﴿١٦﴾

Luqman said: "O my son, indeed if wrong has the weight of a mustard seed and is hidden within a rock or anywhere in the heavens or in the earth, Allah will bring it forth. Indeed, Allah is Subtle and Acquainted." [31:16]

"O my beloved son, do no delay repentance for indeed punishment can come unexpectedly."

وَلَقَدْ ءَاتَيْنَا لُقْمَٰنَ ٱلْحِكْمَةَ أَنِ ٱشْكُرْ لِلَّهِ وَمَن يَشْكُرْ فَإِنَّمَا يَشْكُرُ لِنَفْسِهِۦ وَمَن كَفَرَ فَإِنَّ ٱللَّهَ غَنِيٌّ حَمِيدٌ ﴿١٢﴾

And We had certainly given Luqman wisdom [and said], "Be grateful to Allah." And whoever is grateful is grateful for [the benefit of] himself. And whoever denies [His favor] - then indeed, Allah is Free of need and Praiseworthy. [31:12]

Chapter 2: Al-hamdu-Lillah is the Imbursement of every Favor

Haabib Ibn Al-Shahid reports al-Hassan said: 'al-Hamdu-Lillah is the imbursement of every favor and La iliha il-Allah (there is no God but Allah) is the imbursement for Jannah.'

The meaning of this statement has also been reported from the Prophet (peace and blessings be upon him) on the authority of Abu Dharr, Anas, and many others. Even though the isnads (the list of authorities who have transmitted a report hadith) of all these ahadith contain some weakness, the meaning is also supported by the Quran:

۞ إِنَّ ٱللَّهَ ٱشۡتَرَىٰ مِنَ ٱلۡمُؤۡمِنِينَ أَنفُسَهُمۡ وَأَمۡوَٰلَهُم بِأَنَّ لَهُمُ ٱلۡجَنَّةَ يُقَٰتِلُونَ فِي سَبِيلِ ٱللَّهِ فَيَقۡتُلُونَ وَيُقۡتَلُونَ وَعۡدًا عَلَيۡهِ حَقًّا فِي ٱلتَّوۡرَىٰةِ وَٱلۡإِنجِيلِ وَٱلۡقُرۡءَانِ وَمَنۡ أَوۡفَىٰ بِعَهۡدِهِۦ مِنَ ٱللَّهِ فَٱسۡتَبۡشِرُواْ بِبَيۡعِكُمُ ٱلَّذِي بَايَعۡتُم بِهِۦ وَذَٰلِكَ هُوَ ٱلۡفَوۡزُ ٱلۡعَظِيمُ ﴿١١١﴾

Indeed, Allah has purchased from the believers their lives and their properties [in exchange] for that they will have Paradise. They fight in the cause of Allah, so they kill and are killed. [It is] a true promise [binding] upon Him in the Torah and the Gospel and the Qur'an. And who is truer to his covenant than Allah? So rejoice in your transaction which you have contracted. And it is that which is the great attainment. [9:111]

The Jannah is appointed the imbursement for self and property. The response to this is that Allah, the Glorious and Exalted, through His mercy, beneficence, kindness, and generosity; has addressed His creation in a way that would encourage them to obey Him, using language and concepts that they can easily understand.

Allah, the Wise and Worthy of all Praise, placed Himself in the position of a buyer and debtor, and placed humans in the position of creditors and sellers. This encourages them to answer His call and to rush to His obedience.

In reality, however, everything belongs to Allah and is granted by His grace and mercy: the self and property and everything belong to Allah and this is why Allah commanded us to say at the onset of sadness and calamity:

الَّذِينَ إِذَآ أَصَٰبَتْهُم مُّصِيبَةٌ قَالُوٓاْ إِنَّا لِلَّهِ وَإِنَّآ إِلَيْهِ رَٰجِعُونَ ﴿١٥٦﴾

Who, when disaster strikes them, say, "Indeed we belong to Allah, and indeed to Him we will return." [2:156]

مَآ أَصَابَ مِن مُّصِيبَةٍ إِلَّا بِإِذْنِ ٱللَّهِ وَمَن يُؤْمِنۢ بِٱللَّهِ يَهْدِ قَلْبَهُۥ
وَٱللَّهُ بِكُلِّ شَىْءٍ عَلِيمٌ ﴿١١﴾

No disaster strikes except by permission of Allah. And whoever believes in Allah - He will guide his heart. And Allah is Knowing of all things. [64:11]

All of the deeds come about as a result of His kind grace and mercy, yet He commends those who perform them, attributes the deeds to them, and appoints them to be a show of thanks and gratitude, and return, for His favors.

13

وَإِذْ تَأَذَّنَ رَبُّكُمْ لَئِن شَكَرْتُمْ لَأَزِيدَنَّكُمْ وَلَئِن
كَفَرْتُمْ إِنَّ عَذَابِي لَشَدِيدٌ ﴿٧﴾

And [remember] when your Lord proclaimed: "If you are grateful, I will surely increase you [in favor]; but if you deny, indeed, My punishment is severe." [14:7]

فَاذْكُرُونِي أَذْكُرْكُمْ وَاشْكُرُوا لِي وَلَا تَكْفُرُونِ ﴿١٥٢﴾

Remember Me; I will remember you. And be grateful to Me and do not deny Me. [2:152]

On the authority of Abu-Hurayra, May Allah be pleased with him, he said that the Prophet, peace and blessings be upon him, said: "Allah the Almighty said: I am as My servant thinks of Me. I am with him when he mentions Me. If he makes mention of Me to himself, I will make mention of him to Myself, and if he mentions Me in a gathering, I mention him in a gathering better than it. And if draws near to Me an arm's length, I draw nearer to him. And if he comes to Me walking, I will go to him at speed." [Bukari 7405, Muslim [2675]

Chapter 3: The Meaning of Favors

Ibn Majah records on the authority of Anas that the Prophet (peace and blessings be upon him) said: "There is no favor which Allah bestows upon His creation for which he says, 'al-Hamdu-Lillah,' except that which he gave was better than that which was taken.' This was also stated by Omar Ibn Abdul-Aziz, Al-Hasan, and others from amongst the Salaf.

This has troubled many great number of Islamic scholars, in the past and present, but its meaning is clear and obvious. The meaning of favor mentioned in the hadith is worldly favor, and the statement of praising Allah is one of the religious favors. Religious favors are always better than worldly favors.

The favor of praising Allah has been attributed to the creation (the servant). Allah considers them as giving the greater favor as a return for the original favor (When in reality it is Allah that granted both).

This is why it is mentioned in many narrations, al-Hamdu-Lillah, with a praise that befits and suffices His favors; represses His retribution; and acts as a return for His addition. When understood in this clear light, the statement of praise is the reward of the Jannah (Paradise).

۞ وَسَارِعُوٓاْ إِلَىٰ مَغۡفِرَةٖ مِّن رَّبِّكُمۡ وَجَنَّةٍ عَرۡضُهَا ٱلسَّمَٰوَٰتُ وَٱلۡأَرۡضُ أُعِدَّتۡ لِلۡمُتَّقِينَ ١٣٣

And march forth in the way (which leads to) forgiveness from Allah, and for Paradise as wide as are the heavens and the earth, prepared for Al-Muttaqun (the pious). [3:133]

Chapter 4: Both Paradise & Deeds are from the Grace of Allah

Deeds and Jannah are granted to the believing servants by the grace and mercy of Allah alone. This is why the inhabitants of Jannah will say upon entering it:

وَنَزَعْنَا مَا فِى صُدُورِهِم مِّنْ غِلٍّ تَجْرِى مِن تَحْتِهِمُ ٱلْأَنْهَٰرُ وَقَالُوا۟ ٱلْحَمْدُ لِلَّهِ ٱلَّذِى هَدَىٰنَا لِهَٰذَا وَمَا كُنَّا لِنَهْتَدِىَ لَوْلَآ أَنْ هَدَىٰنَا ٱللَّهُ لَقَدْ جَآءَتْ رُسُلُ رَبِّنَا بِٱلْحَقِّ وَنُودُوٓا۟ أَن تِلْكُمُ ٱلْجَنَّةُ أُورِثْتُمُوهَا بِمَا كُنتُمْ تَعْمَلُونَ ﴿٤٣﴾

"Praise to Allah, who has guided us to this; and we would never have been guided if Allah had not guided us. Certainly the messengers of our Lord had come with the truth." And they will be called, "This is Paradise, which you have been made to inherit for what you used to do." [7:43]

After they acknowledge and understood that it was through the favor of Allah alone that they were granted the Jannah, and that it was through His favor that they were they granted the accord to enact the means leading to it, i.e. His guidance, and after having praised Allah for this, they are rewarded with the call:

وَنَزَعْنَا مَا فِى صُدُورِهِم مِّنْ غِلٍّ تَجْرِى مِن تَحْتِهِمُ الْأَنْهَرُ وَقَالُوا الْحَمْدُ لِلَّهِ الَّذِى هَدَنَا لِهَذَا وَمَا كُنَّا لِنَهْتَدِىَ لَوْلَا أَنْ هَدَنَا اللَّهُ لَقَدْ جَاءَتْ رُسُلُ رَبِّنَا بِالْحَقِّ وَنُودُوا أَن تِلْكُمُ الْجَنَّةُ أُورِثْتُمُوهَا بِمَا كُنتُمْ تَعْمَلُونَ ۞

Behold! This is the Jannah, the Garden you will be made to inherit for all the good deeds. [7:43]

Their deeds were attributed to them and thus they were shown appreciation for them. It is with this overall meaning that some of the Salaf once said: 'when a servant commits a sin and then says: "My Lord, You decreed this for me!"

Allay will say: "You are the one who sinned and disobeyed Me!"

Now if the servant says: "My Lord, please I have erred, and I committed a sin, and wrought evil."

Allah, the Merciful, will respond by saying: "I decreed this upon you and I will forgive you."

Chapter 5: Misery and Felicity Occur through His Justice and Mercy

The true meaning of these words: "Your actions alone will not save any of you." Actions alone will not cause one to enter Jannah. The reward of good deeds, only comes about by the grace of Allah, Merciful. He recompenses a good deed tenfold to seven-hundred (700) fold to whatever Allah wills. [Muslim]

If Allah were to recompense a good deed with its like, in the same way for an evil deed, then good deeds would never have the power to render void (to erase) the evil deeds, and one would surely be destroyed forever.

Ibn Masud once said, while describing good deeds, "If person is an ally (wali) of Allah, and there remain a small atoms weight of good deeds [after the mutual recompense], Allah, the Generous, would increase this manifold such that he enter Jannah through it. [Hakim]

If he be one for whom misery is decreed, the Angel says: "My Lord, His good deeds have all vanished yet many more people remain seeking [mutual recompense]." Allah will reply: "Take their evil deeds and add them to his evil deeds, then prepare for him a place of punishment and torment in the Fire!"

Allah multiplies the good deeds of those He want happiness for until they are able to pay off any penalties [from anyone who seek mutual recompense]. If there remains even an atoms weight worth of good deeds, Allah will multiply this until He enters Jannah through it. All this by Allah's grace and beneficence! However, whoever Allah has decreed misery and punishment for, his deeds will never be multiplied to the extent that they are able to pay off all of his penalties. Instead any good deeds that were performed by this person will only be multiplied ten-fold (10), apportioned amongst his many creditors who will accept them all and yet might still require much more repayment for the many remaining injustices. Therefore their bad deeds will be piled onto his, thereby causing him to fall into the Fire. This by Allah's justice!

It is in this light that Yahiya Ibn Muadh once said: "When Allah extends His beautiful grace, not a single evil deed remains for that person! But when His fair justice is brought forth, not a single good deed remains for that person."

It is also recorded in Muslim and Bukhari that the Prophet (peace and blessings be upon him) said: "Whoever's account is scrutinized will surely be destroyed." [Muslim and Bukhari]

In another narration it is said: "He will be punished," and in another narration: "He will be defeated."

Abu Nuayem records on the authority of Ali that the Prophet (peace and blessings be upon him) have said: "Allah, the Beautiful, the Merciful, revealed to a Prophet amongst the many Prophets of the Children of Israel: 'Say to those who obey Me amongst your people that they should never rely on their good deeds, for on the Day of Judgment I will not settle the accounts of a servant I wish to punish except that I will punish him.

And say to those who disobey me amongst your people that they should not despair and forget Me, for I readily will forgive even the greatest of sins." [Tabarani and Al-Awsat]

Abdul-Aziz Ibn Abu Rawwad said: "Allah inspired Prophet Dawud (David) (peace be upon him) saying: "Dawud, give glad tidings to all sinners and warn those who give in charity."

Very surprised, Prophet Dawud (peace be upon him) said: "My Lord, why should I give happy tidings to the sinners and warn those who give in charity?"

Allah replied: "Give glad tidings to the sinners that there is never a sin that I find too grievous to forgive, and warn those people who give in charity that there is no servant upon whom I dispense My justice and judgment except that he is destroyed."

Ibn Yazid once said: "the easy reckoning is that in which ones sins are forgiven and good deeds are accepted, and the severe reckoning is that which contains no pardoning at all. All of these narrations show us that man can never enter Jannah without the forgiveness and mercy of Allah. The narrations also show us that when Allah passes pure justice upon a servant, that person will surely be destroyed.

Al-Mann (Reminding people of one's favors for them) is a Characteristic of the Miser

يَٰٓأَيُّهَا ٱلَّذِينَ ءَامَنُوا۟ لَا تُبْطِلُوا۟ صَدَقَٰتِكُم بِٱلْمَنِّ وَٱلْأَذَىٰ كَٱلَّذِى يُنفِقُ مَالَهُۥ رِئَآءَ ٱلنَّاسِ وَلَا يُؤْمِنُ بِٱللَّهِ وَٱلْيَوْمِ ٱلْءَاخِرِ فَمَثَلُهُۥ كَمَثَلِ صَفْوَانٍ عَلَيْهِ تُرَابٌ فَأَصَابَهُۥ وَابِلٌ فَتَرَكَهُۥ صَلْدًا لَّا يَقْدِرُونَ عَلَىٰ شَىْءٍ مِّمَّا كَسَبُوا۟ وَٱللَّهُ لَا يَهْدِى ٱلْقَوْمَ ٱلْكَٰفِرِينَ ﴿٢٦٤﴾

O you who have believed, do not invalidate your charities with reminders or injury as does one who spends his wealth only to be seen by the people and does not believe in Allah and the Last Day. His example is like that of a large smooth stone which has dust and is hit by a downpour that leaves it bare. They are unable to keep anything of what they have earned. And Allah does not guide the disbelieving people. [2:264]

There was a Libyan man named Masaud Baaba who used the alms money not only as help for the needy, but also for his purposes and family. Moreover, he constantly reminded others of his favors. Al-Qurtubi, may Allah have mercy upon him, said that reminding others of one's favors for them is always done by a miserly and conceited person.

The miser always feels that what he gave is great, even if it is something insignificant. Also, the conceited person always tends to glorify himself and feels that he is doing others a great favor. The causes for all this are ignorance and forgetfulness of the favors of Allah. If this man had thought carefully, he would have realized that the taker is the one who does him a favor because of the reward that he obtains for giving to him. There are two possible interpretations of reminding others of favors: The first is doing something good for people without boasting. For example, it may be said that someone did another one a favor by rescuing him. The second is when a man keeps reminding people of his favors for them and does this numerous times, to the extent that he destroys fully and squanders what he did.

The first type is excellent and it includes all the favors of Allah that He bestows upon man, but the second one is very bad as it is usually said in order to confirm and announce the favors, or to boast of what one gives until it reaches the poor man. In this case, reminding a person of one's favors is a grave major sin.

There are many Hadeeths, which dispraise the act of reminding people of one's favors. In a Hadeeth on the authority of Abu Tharr, may Allah be pleased with him, the Prophet, peace and blessings be upon him, said: "Allah will not talk to three types of people on the Day of Judgment: the man who gives people things in order to remind them of his favors upon them, the man who sells goods and things and makes false oaths, and the man who allows his lower clothing to hang below his ankles." [Muslim] In a Hadeeth on the authority of Ibn Omar, may Allah be pleased with him, the Prophet, peace and blessings be upon him, said: "Allah will not look at three types of people on the Day of Judgment: the one who is un-dutiful to his mother and father, the woman who imitates men and the Dayyooth (the man who approves of the indecency of his womenfolk, and is void of jealousy).

Moreover, there are three types of people that will never enter Jannah: the one who is undutiful to his mother and father, the one who is addicted to alcohol and drugs, and the one who reminds others of his favors for them. [Al-Albaani – Saheeh, An-Nasaay]

In a Hadeeth on the authority of Abdullaah Ibn Abi-Afwa, may Allah be pleased with him, who said that some of the Arabs said to the Prophet, peace and blessings be upon him. "We reverted to Islam and did not fight you as other tribes did." Hence, the following verse was revealed: [At-Tabaraani, Ibn Mardawayh, and Ibn Al-Munthir with a good chain of narrators]

يَمُنُّونَ عَلَيْكَ أَنْ أَسْلَمُوا۟ قُل لَّا تَمُنُّوا۟ عَلَىَّ إِسْلَـٰمَكُم بَلِ ٱللَّهُ يَمُنُّ عَلَيْكُمْ أَنْ هَدَىٰكُمْ لِلْإِيمَـٰنِ إِن كُنتُمْ صَـٰدِقِينَ ﴿١٧﴾

They consider it a favor to you that they have accepted Islam. Say, "Do not consider your Islam a favor to me. Rather, Allah has conferred favor upon you that He has guided you to the faith, if you should be truthful." [49:17]

In a Hadeeth on the authority of Abu-Bakr, may Allah be pleased with him, the Prophet, peace and blessings be upon him, said: "The deceiver, the person who reminds others of his favors for them, and the miser will not enter Jannah." [Hasan Ghareeb, At-Tirmithi]

It was narrated by Ibn Abu-Haatim said: "No one who reminds others of his favors for them will enter Jannah was truly difficult for me to understand until I found the verses that deal with these type of people in the Quran." Allah the Almighty says:

يَـٰٓأَيُّهَا ٱلَّذِينَ ءَامَنُواْ لَا تُبْطِلُواْ صَدَقَـٰتِكُم بِٱلْمَنِّ وَٱلْأَذَىٰ كَٱلَّذِى يُنفِقُ مَالَهُۥ رِئَآءَ ٱلنَّاسِ وَلَا يُؤْمِنُ بِٱللَّهِ وَٱلْيَوْمِ ٱلْأَخِرِ فَمَثَلُهُۥ كَمَثَلِ صَفْوَانٍ عَلَيْهِ تُرَابٌ فَأَصَابَهُۥ وَابِلٌ فَتَرَكَهُۥ صَلْدًا لَّا يَقْدِرُونَ عَلَىٰ شَىْءٍ مِّمَّا كَسَبُواْ وَٱللَّهُ لَا يَهْدِى ٱلْقَوْمَ ٱلْكَـٰفِرِينَ ﴿٢٦٤﴾

O you who have believed, do not invalidate your charities with reminders or injury as does one who spends his wealth only to be seen by the people and does not believe in Allah and the Last Day. His example is like that of a large smooth stone that has dust and is hit by a downpour that leaves it bare. They are unable [to keep] anything of what they have earned. [2:264]

Abu-Mulaykah Az-Zammaari , may Allah have mercy upon him, said that this refers to the one who reminds others of his favors for them and the arrogant who unlawfully takes people's money through making false oaths.

كَلَّآ إِنَّهُمْ عَن رَّبِّهِمْ يَوْمَئِذٍ لَّمَحْجُوبُونَ ﴿١٥﴾

No! Indeed, from their Lord, that Day, they will be partitioned. [83:15]

Adh-Dhahhaak, may Allah have mercy upon him, said that the one who gives a charity then reminds the taker of his charity or hurts him, would therefore not get a reward. Allah, the Almighty, likens what that person does to a large smooth stone upon which there is dust and which is hit by a downpour that leaves it bare. Allah, the Exalted, removes the reward of the one who reminds people of his charity in the same way the downpour removes the dust of the stone. Reminding people with one's favors for them brings you the wrath of Allah and for being expelled from His mercy. It stirs bitter feelings, invalidates all your good deeds and might even cancel them out totally. Allah will not look at the one who has this ailment, neither will He talk to him on the Day of Judgment. So beware of this illness, as it is a characteristic of miserly people.

Chapter 6: No one can ever repay the Blessings of Allah

ثُمَّ لَتُسْتَلُنَّ يَوْمَبِذٍ عَنِ ٱلنَّعِيمِ ﴿٨﴾

Then, on that Day, you shall be asked about the delight (you indulged in, in this world). [102:8]

This verse shows that the servants will be asked about the pleasures they enjoyed in his life. Did they show gratitude for them or not? Everyone is required to display gratitude for every favor that Allah has bestowed on them, such as good health, eyesight, sound senses, good livelihood, and much more, all of one's good deeds can never repay even some of these favors. Hence that person would be deserving of punishment.

Abdullah Ibn Amr said that the Prophet, peace and blessings be upon him, said: "The servant will be brought on the Day of Judgment, and he will stand before the Mighty and Magnificent. Allah will say to His Angels: "Look at the deeds of My servant and the favors I bestowed upon him." They will look and say: "None amount to one of Your favors granted him."

Allah will say: "Look to his good deeds and evil deeds." They will look and find them the same whereupon, Allah will say: "Servant of Mine, I have accepted your good deeds, and I have forgiven you your evil deeds. My favors, I have gifted to you."

The Tabarani said on the authority of Ibn Omar that the Prophet, peace and blessings be upon him, said: "A person will be brought on the Day of Judgment with a large amount of good deeds that would burden even a mountain if they were to be placed on it! Then just one favor from the favors of Allah would be shown, and that would extinguish all those deeds, but Allah the merciful would accept those deeds, through His mercy." [Tabarani, al-Awsat on the authority of Ibn Omar]

Ibn Abi Al-Dunya records on the authority of Anas that the Prophet, peace and blessings be upon him, said: "On the Day of Judgment, blessings will be brought forward as well as the good deeds and the bad ones. Allah will say to just one of His blessings: 'Take your due from his good deeds,' and it will take all his good deeds."

He also said that Wahb Ibn Munabbih said: A servant once worshipped Allah for 50 years. Allah inspired him with the words: "I have forgiven you." The servant asked: "My Lord, what have you to forgive, I have committed no sins at all!" Thereupon Allah ordered a vein in his neck to throb very painfully such that he could not sleep or pray. But after a few days the pain was removed, and an angel came to him, and the man complained about the pain. The angel said to him: "Allah, the Mighty and Magnificent says: 'Your worship for the last 50 years equates to the soothing of that vein.'" [Abu Nuaym]

Hakim said on the authority of Jabir that the Prophet, peace and blessings be upon him, said: "Jibril said: 'A servant worshipped Allah on the top of a mountain, in the middle of an ocean, for 500 years. Then he asked Allah to let him die in the state of prostration. We used to pass by him, and each time we would descend and ascend, and we would find written in the (pre-eternal knowledge) that the man would be resurrected on the Day of Judgment and would stand before Allah. Then Allah, the Mighty and Magnificent, would say: 'Enter My servant into Jannah by virtue of My mercy.'

The servant will say: 'My Lord, rather by virtue of my deeds!' This will happen 3 times, then Allah will say to His angels: 'Weigh my favors against his deeds,' and they will find that the blessing of sight alone takes up all the deeds he did during his 500 years of worship, with the other bodily blessings still remaining.

Allah will then say: 'Enter My servant into the Fire!'

The man will be dragged towards the Fire and will cry out: 'Enter me into Jannah by virtue of Your mercy! Enter me into Jannah by virtue of Your mercy!' Thereupon he shall enter Jannah." Jibril went on to say: "Muhammad, everything that is good only happen by the mercy of Allah." [Hakim]

Whoever understands all of what has preceded will realize that one's deeds, even if they are too great, are not sufficient enough to merit his success and entry into Jannah or salvation from the Fire in and of themselves.

Ahmad said on the authority of Abi Amirah that the Prophet, peace and blessings be upon him, said: "Were a servant to remain in the state of prostration from the day he was born until the day he dies an old man, in devout obedience to Allah, that would still be very insignificant on the Day of Judgment, and that man would wish to return to this world so that he may increase in reward."

As such, every person should never overly rely on his deeds or be impressed by them, even if they are as big as a mountain. If this is the case of great and many deeds, what then would one think of the worthless deeds of the many? Such a person should think about and consider his deficiency in worship and devote himself to penitence and repentance.

If you fear (does your duty to) Allah He will give you discrimination (or a Criterion) and will rid you of your evil thoughts and deeds, and will forgive you; for Allah is Lord of Infinite Bounty. Ibn Al-Jawazi said:" When true fear of Allah is realized in your heart, all good things will come to you." Allah said: "We will provide for him from where he does not expect.

And whoever relies upon Allah - then He is sufficient for him. Indeed, Allah will accomplish His purpose. Allah has already set for everything a [decreed] extent." [65:3]

وَيَرْزُقْهُ مِنْ حَيْثُ لَا يَحْتَسِبُ وَمَن يَتَوَكَّلْ عَلَى ٱللَّهِ فَهُوَ حَسْبُهُ إِنَّ ٱللَّهَ بَٰلِغُ أَمْرِهِ قَدْ جَعَلَ ٱللَّهُ لِكُلِّ شَىْءٍ قَدْرًا ٣

Allah is with you wherever you are. [57:4]

هُوَ ٱلَّذِى خَلَقَ ٱلسَّمَٰوَٰتِ وَٱلْأَرْضَ فِى سِتَّةِ أَيَّامٍ ثُمَّ ٱسْتَوَىٰ عَلَى ٱلْعَرْشِ يَعْلَمُ مَا يَلِجُ فِى ٱلْأَرْضِ وَمَا يَخْرُجُ مِنْهَا وَمَا يَنزِلُ مِنَ ٱلسَّمَآءِ وَمَا يَعْرُجُ فِيهَا وَهُوَ مَعَكُمْ أَيْنَ مَا كُنتُمْ وَٱللَّهُ بِمَا تَعْمَلُونَ بَصِيرٌ ٤

So fear Allah, and take refuge in Him. He will protect you and will keep evil from reaching you.

Chapter 7: One of the Greatest Blessings is Gratitude

A person whose deeds are many, must show gratitude for them, because gratitude is one of the greatest blessings Allah bestows upon His servant. Wahb Ibn Al-Ward, when asked about the reward of a particular deed, said: "Ask not about the reward, but always ask about the gratitude due upon one who was guided to it."

Abu-Sulayman said: "How can an intelligent person be amazed with his deeds? Deeds are one of Allah's blessings, as such it is upon that person to show gratitude and to show humility. It is only the Qadariyah who are amazed at their deeds!" i.e. those who never believe that the actions of the servant are created by Allah, the Mighty and Magnificent.

How excellent is the words of Abu-Bakr Al-Nahshali on the day that Dawud Al-Tai died. After the burial, Ibn Al-Sammak stood up and praised Dawud for his good deeds and wept causing all present to weep as well and to testify to the truth of what he said.

Abu-Bakr al-Nahshali stood and said: "O Allah, forgive him and show mercy to him and leave him not to his deeds!"

Abu Dawud said on the authority of Zayd Ibn Thabit that the Prophet, peace and blessings be upon him, said: "If Allah wanted to punish His slaves, He could do so without having oppressed them in any way. Were He to show them some mercy, His mercy would be better for them than their deeds." [Ibn Majah and Abu-Dawud]

Hakim said on the authority of Jabir that a man came to the Prophet, peace and blessings be upon him, and said: "Sins, sins! He repeated this 3 times. The Messenger of Allah, peace be upon him, said: "Say: O Allah, Your forgiveness is vaster and mightier than my sins and I have more hope in it than I do my deeds."

عَنْ جَابِرِ بنِ عبد الله قَالَ جَاءَ رَجُلٌ إِلَى النَّبِيِّ صَلَّى اللَّه عَلَيْهِ وَسَلَّمَ فَقَالَ وَاذْنُوبَاهُ وَاذْنُوبَاهُ فَقَالَ لَهُ رَسُولُ اللَّهِ صَلَّى اللَّه عَلَيْهِ وَسَلَّمَ قُلِ اللَّهُمَّ مَغْفِرَتُكَ أَوْسَعُ مِنْ ذُنُوبِي وَرَحْمَتُكَ أَرْجَى عِنْدِي مِنْ عَمَلِي فَقَالَهَا ثُمَّ قَالَ عُدْ فَعَادَ قَالَ ثُمَّ قَالَ عُدْ فَعَادَ قَالَ قُمْ قَدْ غَفَرَ اللَّهُ لَكَ

He said this and the Prophet, peace and blessings be upon him, said: "Repeat it." He did so and he was ordered to repeat it again which he did. Then he, peace and blessings be upon him, said: "Stand! Allah has forgiven you." [Hakim]

On the authority of Abu-Dharr Al-Ghafari, of the Prophet, peace and blessings be upon him, is that among the sayings he relates from Allah, the Merciful, is that He said: "O My servants! I have forbidden oppression for Myself, and I made it forbidden amongst you. Do not oppress one another. O My servants, all of you are astray except those whom I guide, so ask and seek guidance from Me and I shall guide you.

عَنْ أَبِي ذَرٍّ الْغِفَارِيِّ رَضِيَ اللهُ عَنْهُ عَنِ النَّبِيِّ صلى الله عليه و سلم فِيمَا يَرْوِيهِ عَنْ رَبِّهِ تَبَارَكَ وَتَعَالَى، أَنَّهُ قَالَ:

" يَا عِبَادِي: إِنِّي حَرَّمْتُ الظُّلْمَ عَلَى نَفْسِي، وَجَعَلْتُهُ بَيْنَكُمْ مُحَرَّمًا؛ فَلَا تَظَالَمُوا. يَا عِبَادِي! كُلُّكُمْ ضَالٌّ إِلَّا مَنْ هَدَيْتُهُ، فَاسْتَهْدُونِي أَهْدِكُمْ

Chapter 8: Acknowledging the Grace of Allah

Deeds, in and of themselves, do not save you from the Fire or give you entry into Jannah, let alone the ascension to the highest levels of Jannah: the levels of those brought close to Allah's Throne, and seeing the face of Allah, the Mighty and Magnificent. This can only happen through the mercy of Allah, His mercy, grace, and forgiveness. This then requires the believer to abandon and to stop thinking so highly of his deeds. Instead always look solely to the grace of Allah and His blessings.

When this is understood, it is obligatory upon the believing servant to seek Allah's mercy, forgiveness, pleasure, and love. It is in this way that man can attain His generosity. The means are the deeds that Allah has appointed: only those deeds that He has commanded upon the tongue of the Prophet, peace and blessings be upon him. Only those deeds that the Prophet peace and blessings be upon him, told us about that would serve to draw us closer to Allah.

وَلَا تُفۡسِدُوا۟ فِى ٱلۡأَرۡضِ بَعۡدَ إِصۡلَـٰحِهَا وَٱدۡعُوهُ خَوۡفٗا وَطَمَعًا إِنَّ رَحۡمَتَ ٱللَّهِ قَرِيبٞ مِّنَ ٱلۡمُحۡسِنِينَ ۝

And cause not corruption upon the earth after its reformation. And invoke Him in fear and aspiration. Indeed, the mercy of Allah is near to the doers of good. [7:56]

۞ وَٱكۡتُبۡ لَنَا فِى هَـٰذِهِ ٱلدُّنۡيَا حَسَنَةٗ وَفِى ٱلۡأٓخِرَةِ إِنَّا هُدۡنَآ إِلَيۡكَۚ قَالَ عَذَابِىٓ أُصِيبُ بِهِۦ مَنۡ أَشَآءُۖ وَرَحۡمَتِى وَسِعَتۡ كُلَّ شَىۡءٖۚ فَسَأَكۡتُبُهَا لِلَّذِينَ يَتَّقُونَ وَيُؤۡتُونَ ٱلزَّكَوٰةَ وَٱلَّذِينَ هُم بِـَٔايَـٰتِنَا يُؤۡمِنُونَ ۝

Allah said: "My punishment - I afflict with it whom I will, but My mercy encompasses all things." So I will decree it [especially] for those who fear Me and give zakah and those who believe in Our verses. [7:156]

It is obligatory upon the believing servant to seek out those traits of taqwa and goodness that Allah has told us about in His Book or from the Prophet, peace and blessings be upon him, and having done so, this will draw us closer to Allah, the Mighty, the Magnificent, and the Merciful.

Chapter 9: The Most Beloved Deeds to Allah

The Prophet, peace and blessings be upon him, indicated the most beloved of deeds to Allah. They are of two types:

1) Those deeds that are done persistently and continuously, even if it was a simple one rakat prayer at night. The Prophet, peace and be upon him, would prohibit the severance of deeds saying to Abdullah Ibn al-As: "Do not be like such-and-such man who used to pray by night and then left it." [Muslim and Bukhari]

The Prophet, peace and blessings be upon him, said: "The supplication of one of you will be answered, but be patient. Never say I have supplicated and supplicated but have not been answered, so the person despairs and then abandons the supplication." [Muslim and Bukhari]

Al-Hasan said: "When Shaytan (Satan) looks at you and sees that you are persistent in your obedience to Allah, Mighty and Magnificent, he will do his utmost to stop and to deceive you. If the Shaytan still sees you persistent, he will get tired of you and leave. However, if the Shaytan sees that you are alternating between this and that, he will have try his best to destroy you."

قَالَ فَبِمَا أَغْوَيْتَنِى لَأَقْعُدَنَّ لَهُمْ صِرَٰطَكَ ٱلْمُسْتَقِيمَ ﴿١٦﴾

(Shaytan) said: "Because You have sent me astray, surely I will sit in wait against them (human beings) on Your Straight Path. [7:16]

إِنَّ عِبَادِى لَيْسَ لَكَ عَلَيْهِمْ سُلْطَٰنٌ وَكَفَىٰ بِرَبِّكَ وَكِيلًا ﴿٦٥﴾

Allah said: Indeed, over My [believing] servants there is for you no authority. And sufficient is your Lord as Disposer of affairs." [17:65]

Ibn Taymiyyah, may Allah have mercy on him, said: "If a shepherd's dog ever attempts to attack you, do not engage it in a fight. Instead seek the shepherd's help. He will leash it and save you the fight."

So when the Shaytan tries to harm you, take refuge in Allah the Almighty. Allah will protect you and will keep the Shaytan away from you.

2) Allah, the Merciful, loves those deeds that are done with steadiness, balance, and ease rather than those that cause hardship. Allah, Exalted is He, says in the Quran:

$$\text{اَللّٰهُ بِكُمُ ٱلۡيُسۡرَ وَلَا يُرِيدُ بِكُمُ ٱلۡعُسۡرَ وَلِتُكۡمِلُوا۟ ٱلۡعِدَّةَ وَلِتُكَبِّرُوا۟ ٱللّٰهَ عَلَىٰ مَا هَدَىٰكُمۡ وَلَعَلَّكُمۡ تَشۡكُرُونَ ۝١٨٥}$$

Allah desires ease for you. The Merciful desires not hardship for you. [2:185]

$$\text{مَا يُرِيدُ ٱللّٰهُ لِيَجۡعَلَ عَلَيۡكُم مِّنۡ حَرَجٍ وَلَٰكِن يُرِيدُ لِيُطَهِّرَكُمۡ وَلِيُتِمَّ نِعۡمَتَهُۥ عَلَيۡكُمۡ لَعَلَّكُمۡ تَشۡكُرُونَ ۝٦}$$

Allah does not intend to make difficulty for you, but He intends to purify you and complete His favor upon you that you may be grateful. [5:6]

وَجَـٰهِدُواْ فِى ٱللَّهِ حَقَّ جِهَادِهِۦ هُوَ ٱجْتَبَـٰكُمْ وَمَا جَعَلَ عَلَيْكُمْ فِى ٱلدِّينِ مِنْ حَرَجٍ مِّلَّةَ أَبِيكُمْ إِبْرَٰهِيمَ هُوَ سَمَّـٰكُمُ ٱلْمُسْلِمِينَ مِن قَبْلُ وَفِى هَـٰذَا لِيَكُونَ ٱلرَّسُولُ شَهِيدًا عَلَيْكُمْ وَتَكُونُواْ شُهَدَآءَ عَلَى ٱلنَّاسِ فَأَقِيمُواْ ٱلصَّلَوٰةَ وَءَاتُواْ ٱلزَّكَوٰةَ وَٱعْتَصِمُواْ بِٱللَّهِ هُوَ مَوْلَىٰكُمْ فَنِعْمَ ٱلْمَوْلَىٰ وَنِعْمَ ٱلنَّصِيرُ ۝ ٧٨

And strive for Allah with the striving due to Him. He has chosen you and has not placed upon you in the religion any difficulty. [It is] the religion of your father, Abraham. Allah named you "Muslims" before [in former scriptures] and in this [revelation] that the Messenger may be a witness over you and you may be witnesses over the people. So establish prayer and give zakah and hold fast to Allah. He is your protector; and excellent is the protector, and excellent is the helper. [22:78]

The Prophet, peace be upon him, would say: "Try to make things easy and do not make them difficult." [Muslim and Bukhari]

The Prophet, peace and blessing be upon him, said: "You have been sent to them to make things easy. You have not been sent to make things difficult." [Abu-Dawud and Bukhari]

Ahmad records on the authority of Ibn Abbas that it was asked of the Prophet, peace and blessings be upon him, "which of the religions is most beloved to Allah?' The Prophet, peace and blessings be upon him, said: "The easy and natural religion." [Ahmad and Bukhari]

Ahmad records on the authority of Mihjan Ibn Al-Adra that the Prophet, peace and blessings be upon him, entered the Masjid and saw a man standing in prayer. The Prophet asked: "Do you think him to be truthful?" It was said: "Prophet of Allah, this man is so-and-so. He is the best of the residents of Madinah, and the most frequent of the people in prayer!" The Prophet, peace and blessings be upon him, said: "Do not let him hear you lest you render him to ruin. The Prophet, peace and blessings be upon him, said it 3 times - you are a nation from whom ease is desired." [Ahmad]

In other narrations, "The best part of your religion is the easiest of it." "You will not attain this matter by excess and trying to overcome it." [Ahmad]

This Hadith was also recorded by Humyad Ibn Zanjaway and his version adds the following: "do such actions as long as you are able to bear. Allah, the Merciful, will not stop rewarding you until you grow tired and stop, and upon you is a journey to Allah at the beginning of each day, at the end of the day, and the last part of the night." [Bukhari]

Ahmad records on the authority of Buraydah who said: "I went out only to see the Prophet, peace and blessings be upon him, so I walked along with him. We then saw a man in front of us praying many prayers and the Prophet, peace and blessings be upon him, asked: "Do you think he is showing off?" I said: "Allah and His Messenger know best." The Prophet, peace and blessings be upon him, then said: "Stick to a middle path always, for whoever makes this religion difficult will find that it will overwhelm him." [Ahmad]

The Prophet, peace and blessings be upon him, objected to those who want to continuously live a life of a hermit, praying through the whole night, fast each day, and recite the whole Quran every night. The Prophet, peace and blessings be upon him, said: "I fast, and I break my fast; I pray by night and I sleep; and I marry women: whoever turns away from my Sunnah is not of me." [Abu-Dawud]

The Prophet, peace and blessings be upon him, advised Abdullah Ibn Amr to recite the Quran completely every 7 days, and another narration mentions that he advised him to complete it once every 3 days. The Prophet, peace be upon him, said, "The one who recites it in less than 3 days has not read it carefully and understood it." With regards fasting, the Prophet, peace and blessing be upon him, finally him with the fast of Dawud saying: "There is no fast better than that." With regards praying by night, the Prophet, peace and blessings be upon him, advised with the prayer of Prophet Dawud, peace be upon him. [Muslim and Bukhari]

Ibn Taymiyyah, may Allah have mercy on his soul, said: "Verily, I constantly renew my Islam until this very day, as up to now, I do not consider myself to have ever been a good Muslim."

Ibn Taymiyyah is one of the great scholars of Islam, yet his humble nature and fear of Allah are depicted here. One should not depend on their deeds, and must continuously strive to do better.

وَلَا تَمْشِ فِي الْأَرْضِ مَرَحًا إِنَّكَ لَن تَخْرِقَ الْأَرْضَ وَلَن تَبْلُغَ الْجِبَالَ طُولًا ٣٧

And do not walk upon the earth exultantly. Indeed, you will never tear the earth [apart], and you will never reach the mountains in height. [17:37]

Chapter 10: The Meaning of "Saddidu wa Qaribu"

Abu-Hurayrah and Aishah reported that the Prophet, peace and blessings be upon him, said: "Be firm, steadfast, and balanced always, [Saddidu wa Qaribu]."

Saddidu means be moderate. Act with fortitude and firmness. Take a balanced path in worship. Do not be deficient in what Allah has ordered, and do not take on more than you can endure. Take the path of balance in the religion. Qaribu means the same thing. Take a middle path between excessiveness and deficiency. The Prophet, peace and blessings be upon him, said: "Stick to a middle path. Upon which have glad tidings," which means that whoever obeys Allah upon firmness and balance, for him are glad tidings. He will reach the goal and he will outstrip the one who expends a lot of effort in performing deeds. The path of balance and firmness is far better than all other paths; being balanced following the Sunnah of the Prophet, peace and blessing be upon him, is better than striving hard in other than it. The best guidance is the guidance of the Prophet." [Muslim]

Whoever traverses the middle path will find it closer to Allah than any other path. Virtue is never attained by doing a great deal of outward deeds. Virtue is attained by deeds being sincere for Allah and doing them correctly in that they are done in accordance to the Sunnah of the Prophet, peace and blessings be upon him.

Whoever has more knowledge of religion and of Allah's ordinances, and has more hope, fear, and love for Allah is far better than one who has not attained his level, even if the latter is doing more outward deeds. This understanding came from the hadith of Aishah: "Be steadfast, firm, and balanced upon which have glad tidings, for deeds alone will not cause one to enter Jannah. The most beloved deeds to Allah are the deeds that are done persistently and continuously, even if they are few."

Some of the Salaf said: "Abu-Bakr did not outdo you by virtue of much prayer and fasting, but rather because of something that had taken root in Abu-Bakr's heart." [Hakim & Tirmidhi] Some of them said: "What was in the heart of Abu-Bakr was the love of Allah the Almighty, and sincerity to His servants."

Many of the Gnostics said: "None who reached the heights did so through a great deal of prayer and fasting, but rather through soundness of heart, generosity of soul, and sincerity to the Allah." Others also added: "and censure of their own souls." Some of them said: "The difference in their ranking and position lay in their intent and objectives, and not in a great deal of prayer and fasting."

The long life of the children of Israel and their great efforts in worship and prayer was told to Abu- Sulayman to which he said: "Allah the Almighty wants from His slaves only a truthful intention for what lies with Him." Ibn Masud said to his companions: "You pray and fast far more than the Companions of Muhammad, peace and blessings be upon him, but they were still better than you." They asked, "How so?" Ibn Masud said: "They were more abstinent of this life and more desirous of the Hereafter." The superiority of the Companions of the Prophet lay in the attachment of their hearts to Allah and the Hereafter, their longing for the Hereafter, their turning away from this world, and their thinking very little of this life even if it be readily available to them.

Companions' hearts were empty of this life and filled with the Hereafter. This is what they inherited from Prophet Muhammad, peace and blessings be upon him. The Prophet, peace and blessings be upon him, was one whose heart was most devoid of this life and most attached to Allah and the afterlife. This was also the state of the Khulafah who came after him and those who followed them in goodness such as Omar Ibn Abdul-Aziz and al-Hasan. There were, in their times, those people who prayed and fasted more than them, but their hearts did not attain the levels of theirs in terms of leaving the life and turning to the afterlife.

A man came to al-Hasan al-Basri, may Allah have mercy on him, and said: "I complain to you of the hardness of my heart!" Al-Hasan said: Discipline your it with *dhiker of Allah.*"

$$\text{ٱلَّذِينَ ءَامَنُوا۟ وَتَطۡمَئِنُّ قُلُوبُهُم بِذِكۡرِ ٱللَّهِ ۗ أَلَا بِذِكۡرِ ٱللَّهِ تَطۡمَئِنُّ ٱلۡقُلُوبُ ۝}$$

Those who have believed and whose hearts are assured by the remembrance of Allah. Unquestionably, by the remembrance of Allah hearts are assured. [13:28]

ٱلَّذِينَ ءَامَنُواْ وَعَمِلُواْ ٱلصَّٰلِحَٰتِ طُوبَىٰ لَهُمْ وَحُسْنُ مَـَٔابٍ ۝

Those who have believed and done righteous deeds - a good state is theirs and a good return. [13:29]

كَذَٰلِكَ أَرْسَلْنَٰكَ فِىٓ أُمَّةٍ قَدْ خَلَتْ مِن قَبْلِهَآ أُمَمٌ لِّتَتْلُوَاْ عَلَيْهِمُ ٱلَّذِىٓ أَوْحَيْنَآ إِلَيْكَ وَهُمْ يَكْفُرُونَ بِٱلرَّحْمَٰنِ قُلْ هُوَ رَبِّى لَآ إِلَٰهَ إِلَّا هُوَ عَلَيْهِ تَوَكَّلْتُ وَإِلَيْهِ مَتَابِ ۝

Thus have We sent you to a community before which [other] communities have passed on so you might recite to them that which We revealed to you, while they disbelieve in the Most Merciful. Say, "He is my Lord; there is no deity except Him. Upon Him I rely, and to Him is my return." [13:30]

Chapter 11: A Noble Principle

The best of people are those who walk the path of the Prophet, peace and blessings be upon him. The Prophet, peace and blessing be upon him, and his Companions were moderate in the bodily actions of worship and strived to correct the states and affairs of their heart. The journey to the afterlife is cut short by the journey of the heart.

$$رَبَّنَا لَا تُزِغْ قُلُوبَنَا بَعْدَ إِذْ هَدَيْتَنَا وَهَبْ لَنَا مِن لَّدُنكَ رَحْمَةً إِنَّكَ أَنتَ الْوَهَّابُ ﴿٨﴾$$

Our Lord, let not our hearts deviate after You have guided us and grant us from Yourself mercy. Indeed, You are the Bestower. [3:8]

A man came to one of the Gnostics and he said: "I took a very difficult journey to reach you." He replied: "The matter is not about difficult and arduous journeys, but with one step, distance your lower self from you and then will you find the completion of your objective."

Abu-Zayd said: "I saw Allah in a dream and I asked Him: "My Lord! How can I traverse the path to You?" He replied: "Abandon yourself and come with welcome!" [Sifatul Safwah, Ibn al-Jawzi]

No previous nation has been given what our nation has been given and that by virtue of its following its Prophet, peace and blessings be upon him. The Prophet, peace and blessings be upon him, was the best of all of creation and his guidance was the best of guidance, through the Prophet, peace and blessings be upon him, Allah made our religion easy, and through him He unburdened our nation of many difficulties. Whoever obeys the Messenger of Allah, peace and blessings be upon him, has obeyed Allah the Almighty, and followed His guidance, and Allah will, in turn, love him.

Ibn Al-Qayyim, may Allah have mercy on him, said: "If Allah wants well for His servant, Allah will strip away from his heart the ability to see his own good deeds and to speak about them with his tongue. Allah will preoccupy him with seeing his sins and they will continue to remain in front of his own eyes until he enters Jannah.

Chapter 12: The Ease of this Religion

Some examples of the ease that came through the Prophet's blessings is that the person that prays Isha in congregation, it is as if he has prayed half the night. Moreover, the one who prays Fajr in congregation, it is as if he has prayed the entire night. [Muslim]

Hence the night prayer is written in his record while he lies asleep. And whoever fasts 3 days of every month it is as if he has fasted the entire month. [Muslim and Bukhari]

أَمَّنْ هُوَ قَنِتٌ ءَانَآءَ ٱلَّيۡلِ سَاجِدًا وَقَآئِمًا يَحۡذَرُ ٱلۡأٓخِرَةَ وَيَرۡجُواْ رَحۡمَةَ رَبِّهِۦ قُلۡ هَلۡ يَسۡتَوِى ٱلَّذِينَ يَعۡلَمُونَ وَٱلَّذِينَ لَا يَعۡلَمُونَ إِنَّمَا يَتَذَكَّرُ أُوْلُواْ ٱلۡأَلۡبَٰبِ ۝

Is one who is devoutly obedient during periods of the night, prostrating and standing [in prayer], fearing the Hereafter and hoping for the mercy of his Lord, [like one who does not]? Say, "Are those who know equal to those who do not know?" Only they will remember [who are] people of understanding. [39:9]

Whoever has the intention of waking up to pray at night but is overcome by sleep will still have the reward of the night prayer recorded for him, and that sleep would be as a charity from Allah. [Ibn Majah and Abu-Dawud]

وَمِنَ ٱلَّيۡلِ فَتَهَجَّدۡ بِهِۦ نَافِلَةً لَّكَ عَسَىٰٓ أَن يَبۡعَثَكَ رَبُّكَ مَقَامًا مَّحۡمُودًا ﴿٧٩﴾

And from [part of] the night, pray with it as additional [worship] for you; it is expected that your Lord will resurrect you to a praised station. [17:79]

كَانُواْ قَلِيلٗا مِّنَ ٱلَّيۡلِ مَا يَهۡجَعُونَ ﴿١٧﴾

They used to sleep but little by night [invoking their Lord (Allah) and praying, with fear and hope]. [51:17]

Someone said: "Many are the ones seeking and wanting forgiveness but their lot is anger, and many are the ones who are often silent but their lot is mercy. The first one seeks and wants forgiveness but his heart remains the heart of a sinner. However, the second one often remains silent but his heart is always engrossed in the remembrance of Allah the Almighty."

Chapter 13: Prayer sets the rhythm of the day

The Prophet, peace and blessings be upon him, said: "Journey to Allah in the beginning of each day, at the end of the day, and a portion of the latter part of the night." In another narration: "Seek help from Allah by journeying to Allah at the beginning of the day, at the end of the day, and a portion of the latter part of the night."

These three periods are times to worship Allah and by doing actions of obedience. These are the beginning of the day, the end of the day, and at the end of the night. Allah the Almighty, mentioned these three times in the Quran:

وَاذْكُرِ اسْمَ رَبِّكَ بُكْرَةً وَأَصِيلًا ﴿٢٥﴾

And mention the name of your Lord [in prayer] morning and evening. [76:25]

وَمِنَ الَّيْلِ فَاسْجُدْ لَهُ وَسَبِّحْهُ لَيْلًا طَوِيلًا ﴿٢٦﴾

And during the night prostrate to Him and exalt Him a long [part of the] night. [76:26]

فَٱصۡبِرۡ عَلَىٰ مَا يَقُولُونَ وَسَبِّحۡ بِحَمۡدِ رَبِّكَ قَبۡلَ طُلُوعِ ٱلشَّمۡسِ وَقَبۡلَ غُرُوبِهَا وَمِنۡ ءَانَآيِ ٱلَّيۡلِ فَسَبِّحۡ وَأَطۡرَافَ ٱلنَّهَارِ لَعَلَّكَ تَرۡضَىٰ ﴿١٣٠﴾

So bear patiently what they say, and glorify the praises of your Lord before the rising of the sun, and before its setting, and during some of the hours of the night, and at the sides of the day (an indication for the five compulsory congregational prayers), that you may become pleased with the reward which Allah shall give you. [20:130]

فَٱصۡبِرۡ عَلَىٰ مَا يَقُولُونَ وَسَبِّحۡ بِحَمۡدِ رَبِّكَ قَبۡلَ طُلُوعِ ٱلشَّمۡسِ وَقَبۡلَ ٱلۡغُرُوبِ ﴿٣٩﴾

وَمِنَ ٱلَّيۡلِ فَسَبِّحۡهُ وَأَدۡبَٰرَ ٱلسُّجُودِ ﴿٤٠﴾

So bear with patience all that they say, and glorify the Praises of your Lord, before the rising of the sun and before its setting. And during a part of the night also, glorify His praises, and so likewise after the prayers. [50:39-40]

Allah, Most High, mentions in the Quran the remembrance of Him at the two ends of the day in numerous places in His Book such as:

يَٰٓأَيُّهَا ٱلَّذِينَ ءَامَنُوا۟ ٱذْكُرُوا۟ ٱللَّهَ ذِكْرًا كَثِيرًا ﴿٤١﴾

وَسَبِّحُوهُ بُكْرَةً وَأَصِيلًا ﴿٤٢﴾

O you who believe! Remember Allah with much remembrance, and glorify His Praises morning and afternoon [the early morning (Fajr) and Asr prayers]. [33:41-42]

فَٱصْبِرْ إِنَّ وَعْدَ ٱللَّهِ حَقٌّ وَٱسْتَغْفِرْ لِذَنۢبِكَ وَسَبِّحْ بِحَمْدِ رَبِّكَ بِٱلْعَشِيِّ وَٱلْإِبْكَٰرِ ﴿٥٥﴾

Be patient. Verily, the Promise of Allah is true, and ask forgiveness for your fault, and glorify the praises of your Lord in the Ashi (i.e. the time period after the midnoon till sunset) and in the Ibkar (i.e. the time period from early morning or sunrise till before midnoon) [it is said that, that means the five compulsory congregational Salat (prayers) or the Asr and Fajr prayers]. [40:55]

وَلَا تَطْرُدِ ٱلَّذِينَ يَدْعُونَ رَبَّهُم بِٱلْغَدَوٰةِ وَٱلْعَشِيِّ يُرِيدُونَ وَجْهَهُۥ مَا عَلَيْكَ مِنْ حِسَابِهِم مِّن شَىْءٍ وَمَا مِنْ حِسَابِكَ عَلَيْهِم مِّن شَىْءٍ فَتَطْرُدَهُمْ فَتَكُونَ مِنَ ٱلظَّٰلِمِينَ ۝

And turn not away those who invoke their Lord, morning and afternoon seeking His Face. You are accountable for them in nothing, and they are accountable for you in nothing, that you may turn them away, and thus become of the Zalimun (unjust). [6:52]

Allah, the Mighty and Magnificent, mentions in the Quran about the remembrance of Prophet Zakariyyah, peace be upon him:

فَخَرَجَ عَلَىٰ قَوْمِهِۦ مِنَ ٱلْمِحْرَابِ فَأَوْحَىٰٓ إِلَيْهِمْ أَن سَبِّحُوا بُكْرَةً وَعَشِيًّا ۝

Then he came out to his people from Al-Mihrab (a praying place or a private room, etc.), he told them by signs to glorify Allah's Praises in the morning and in the afternoon. [19:11]

قَالَ رَبِّ اجْعَل لِّيَ ءَايَةً قَالَ ءَايَتُكَ أَلَّا تُكَلِّمَ النَّاسَ ثَلَثَةَ أَيَّامٍ إِلَّا رَمْزًا وَاذْكُر رَّبَّكَ كَثِيرًا وَسَبِّحْ بِالْعَشِيِّ وَالْإِبْكَرِ ﴿٤١﴾

"... And remember your Lord much and exalt [Him with praise] in the evening and the morning." [3:41]

Out of these 3 times there are two which are at the beginning of the day and the end of the day. At these 2 times one finds both obligatory and optional prayers to do. The obligatory prayers are the prayers of Fajr and Asr and these two are the best prayers of the 5 daily prayers, and whoever preserves these two prayers shall enter Jannah. As for the optional good deeds, is to remember Allah after the Fajr prayer until the sun rises, and after Asr until the sun sets. [Muslim and Bukhari]

Likewise there are many texts concerning the remembrances to be said in the morning and evening and concerning the excellence of one who remembers Allah when awaking and when sleeping.

Ibn Omar reports that the Messenger of Allah, peace and blessings be upon him said: "Son of Adam, remember me for an hour in the beginning of each day and an hour at the end of each day, and I will forgive you your sins committed between these times save any major sins for which you must repent." [Abu-Nuaym]

The first three generations of Muslims (Salaf) placed a greater emphasis on the end of the day than the beginning. Ibn Al-Mubarak said: "It has reached us that anyone who remembers Allah at the end of the day will be recorded as having performed remembrance throughout the day." And Abul-Jald said: "It has reached us that Allah the Almighty, descends to the lowest heavens during the eve of each day and looks at the deeds of the children of Adam."

One of the Salaf saw Abu-Jafar Al-Qari in a dream and he said to him: "Tell Abu-Hazim Al-Araj that Allah and His Angels look to your gathering in the evenings." [Ibn Al-Jawzi] Abu-Hazim used to narrate stories to people at the end of each day.

A Hadith mentions that remembrance after Fajr prayer is more beloved than freeing 4 slaves, and remembrance after Asr prayer is better than freeing 8 slaves. [Ahmad]

The end of the day of Jumuah is better than its beginning because it has an hour wherein the supplication is answered by Allah. [Muslim and Bukhari]

The end of the Day of Arafah (Hajj) is better than the beginning because the end of the day is the time of standing. The end of each night is far better than the beginning of the night as was stated by the Salaf, and they presented the hadith of the Descent as proof. All of these facts strengthen and supports the opinion of those who say that Asr is the "Middle Prayer."

The third period is the duljah (journeying in the last part of the night). The meaning here is praying and doing deeds at the end of the night. This is the time for asking for forgiveness.

Allah, Exalted is He says:

$$\text{ٱلصَّٰبِرِينَ وَٱلصَّٰدِقِينَ وَٱلۡقَٰنِتِينَ وَٱلۡمُنفِقِينَ وَٱلۡمُسۡتَغۡفِرِينَ بِٱلۡأَسۡحَارِ ١٧}$$

The patient, the true, the obedient, those who spend [in the way of Allah], *and those who seek forgiveness before dawn.* [3:17]

$$\text{وَبِٱلۡأَسۡحَارِ هُمۡ يَسۡتَغۡفِرُونَ ١٨}$$

And in the hours before dawn they would ask forgiveness. [51:18]

The period referred to in these verses (before dawn) is the last part of the time of the Descent in which Allah fulfils the prayers of the servants and also grants forgiveness to the penitent.

Some narrations mention that Allah's Throne quivers before Dawn, before the last part of the night. Tawus said: "I cannot understand why anyone would sleep during the last part of the night, when Allah has come to you to help."

In a Hadith recorded by Tirmidhi, he said: "Whoever is afraid should travel by night, and whoever travels by night, Inshallah, will reach his destination." [Hakim and Tirmidhi]

Traveling in the last part of the night cuts short the journey of the Hereafter and the world as is mentioned in the Hadith by Muslim: "When you journey, travel at the end of the night, for the earth is compacted during that night time." [Abu-Dawud]

It is reported that Al-Ashtar entered upon Ali Ibn Abu-Talib, may Allah have mercy on him, after resting part of the night he found Ali standing in prayer. He said: "Leader of the Believers, praying each night, fasting each day, and hard at work during the two!"

When Ali had finished praying, he said: "The journey to the Hereafter is very long, and we need to cut short it by journeying by night," - this is the duljah!

The wife of Habib (Abu Mohammad Al-Farisi), would wake him at night time and she would say: "Awake O Habib for the road is very long and our provision is very paltry. The caravan of the righteous has passed way ahead of us and we have been left far behind!"

Omar Al-khattab, may Allah have mercy on him, said: "The Messenger of Allah, peace and blessing be upon him, said: "Actions are to be judged only by intentions and a man will have only what he intended."

وَمِنَ ٱلَّيْلِ فَتَهَجَّدْ بِهِۦ نَافِلَةً لَّكَ عَسَىٰٓ أَن يَبْعَثَكَ رَبُّكَ مَقَامًا مَّحْمُودًا ﴿٧٩﴾

And from [part of] the night, pray with it as additional [worship] for you; it is expected that your Lord will resurrect you (raise thee) to a praised station. [17:79]

أَمَّنْ هُوَ قَنِتٌ ءَانَآءَ ٱلَّيْلِ سَاجِدًا وَقَآئِمًا يَحْذَرُ ٱلْأَخِرَةَ وَيَرْجُوا۟ رَحْمَةَ رَبِّهِ قُلْ هَلْ يَسْتَوِى ٱلَّذِينَ يَعْلَمُونَ وَٱلَّذِينَ لَا يَعْلَمُونَ إِنَّمَا يَتَذَكَّرُ أُو۟لُوا۟ ٱلْأَلْبَبِ ۩

Is one who is devoutly obedient during periods of the night, prostrating and standing [in prayer], fearing the Hereafter and hoping for the mercy of his Lord, [like one who does not]? [39:19]

كَانُوا۟ قَلِيلًا مِّنَ ٱلَّيْلِ مَا يَهْجَعُونَ ۩

They used to sleep but little by night [invoking their Lord (Allah) and praying, with fear and hope]. [51:17]

قُمِ ٱلَّيْلَ إِلَّا قَلِيلًا ۩

Stand (to pray) all night, except a little. [73:2]

Chapter 14: The Meaning of Moderation

The Prophet, peace and blessing be upon him, said: "Moderation! Moderation! And through this will you attain Al-Jannah!" Moderation in worship and avoid excess and deficiency. It is for this reason that the Prophet, peace and blessings be upon him, repeated it twice. Al-Bazzar recorded the hadith on the authority of Hudhayyfah that the Prophet, peace and blessings be upon him said: "Excellent indeed is moderation in poverty! Excellent indeed is moderation in affluence! Excellent indeed is moderation in worship!"

Mutarraf ibn Shikhkhir had a son who would struggle greatly in worship so he said to his son: "The best of affairs is the middle one. The good deed lies between two evil deeds. The poorest of journeys is the one where one struggle much, he kills his mount and so he is left stranded." [Baihaqi]

Abu-Ubaydah said: "Excessiveness in worship is evil, and deficiency is evil, but moderation is praiseworthy."

This meaning is also supported by the hadith reported on the authority of Abdullah Ibn Amr. The Prophet, peace and blessings be upon him, said: "This religion is powerful. Walk in it with gentleness. Do not let the worship of Allah become so burdensome for you for the one who is unable to continue has neither reduced the journey or preserved his mount. Work the deeds of a man that believes that he will die as an old man, and fear the man who believes that he will die the next day." [Ibn Zanjawayh]

The Prophet, peace be upon him, repeatedly mentioned moderation, which indicates that one must persist in this moderation. This is because any strenuous journey in which one struggles greatly is prone to end very suddenly without completion. However, with a moderate journey, it is more likely to reach the goal. This is why the Prophet, peace and blessings be upon him, said that the result of moderation is to achieve the objective, and whoever journeys by night will reach the destination.

يَٰٓأَيُّهَا ٱلْإِنسَٰنُ إِنَّكَ كَادِحٌ إِلَىٰ رَبِّكَ كَدْحًا فَمُلَٰقِيهِ ﴿٦﴾

O mankind, indeed you are laboring toward your Lord with [great] exertion and will meet it. [84:6]

وَٱعْبُدْ رَبَّكَ حَتَّىٰ يَأْتِيَكَ ٱلْيَقِينُ ﴿٩٩﴾

And worship your Lord until there comes to you the certainty (death). [15:99]

Al-Hasan once said to the people: "Persistence, persistence! Surely Allah has appointed the time of cessation of good deeds to be just before death." Al-Hasan then recited the above verse from the Quran. He also said: "Your souls are your mounts. Therefore, tend to your mounts, in this way they will convey you to your Creator, the Mighty and Magnificent."

The meaning to tend to one's mounts is to be easy on them. So keep them fit and healthy, and do not overburden them. Therefore if you feel your soul is coming to a halt, a stop, during the journey, then tend to it by instilling in it the desire to finish the journey, or by instilling in it the fear of not completing the journey.

One of the Salaf once said: "Hope is the guide. Fear is the driver. The soul is between the two like a head strong animal." If the guide grows tired and the driver is unable to do anything, the soul would then stop. It would then need gentle and kind treatment to provoke it into continuing the journey.

Fear is exactly like a whip. When a shepherd whips the animal excessively, it could well stop and die. Therefore one must rather strike it with songs of kindness and hope that might encourage it to eagerly regenerate its efforts until it arrives at the intended destination.

Abu-Yazid said: "I have persistently guided and directed my soul to Allah without letting up. It wept all the way, but I urged it on until it smiled and laughed."

Chapter 15: Travelling the Path of Allah, Mighty and Magnificent

Khulayid Al-Asari said: "Every person wants to meet his beloved, so love Allah alone and travel to Him with a fine journey: neither arduous nor lax. This journey will take a good believer to his Creator and whoever does not know the path then will not reach it, and there is no difference between such a person and an animal."

Prophet Yunus, peace be upon him, said: "The lowly are those people who do not know the path to their Lord, and nor do they try or seek to know it."

The fine path to Allah is to traverse His Straight Path with which He sent the Prophet, peace and blessings be upon him, and for which He revealed in His Quran. It is this fine Path that He commanded all of mankind to traverse. Ibn Masud said: "The Straight Path is the path that the Prophet, peace and blessings be upon him, left us on, one end of it is here and the other end is in al-Jannah.

To its right and left are other paths branches that summons the people. However, whoever takes those paths will end up in the Fire. The person who remains on the Straight Path will end up in al-Jannah."

The Prophet, peace and blessing be upon him, recited:

وَأَنَّ هَٰذَا صِرَٰطِى مُسۡتَقِيمًا فَٱتَّبِعُوهُ وَلَا تَتَّبِعُواْ ٱلسُّبُلَ فَتَفَرَّقَ بِكُمۡ عَن سَبِيلِهِۦۚ ذَٰلِكُمۡ وَصَّىٰكُم بِهِۦ لَعَلَّكُمۡ تَتَّقُونَ ١٥٣

This is My path, which is straight, so follow it; and do not follow [other] ways, for you will be separated from His way. This has He instructed you that you may become righteous. [6:153]

This was also recorded by Ibn Jarir and others. The Path that leads to Allah and to al-Jannah, is the Straight Path. All other paths are the paths of the Shaytan, and whoever traverses those paths is cut off from Allah forever, and will end up in the Fire, the abode of Allah's displeasure, anger, and painful punishment.

اَهْدِنَا الصِّرَاطَ الْمُسْتَقِيمَ ۝

Guide us to the straight path. [1:6]

سَيَقُولُ السُّفَهَآءُ مِنَ النَّاسِ مَا وَلَّىٰهُمْ عَن قِبْلَتِهِمُ الَّتِى كَانُوا عَلَيْهَا ۚ قُل لِّلَّهِ الْمَشْرِقُ وَالْمَغْرِبُ ۚ يَهْدِى مَن يَشَآءُ إِلَىٰ صِرَٰطٍ مُّسْتَقِيمٍ ۝

The foolish among the people will say, "What has turned them away from their qiblah, which they used to face?" Say, "To Allah belongs the east and the west. He guides whom He wills to a straight path." [2:142]

كَانَ النَّاسُ أُمَّةً وَٰحِدَةً فَبَعَثَ اللَّهُ النَّبِيِّنَ مُبَشِّرِينَ وَمُنذِرِينَ وَأَنزَلَ مَعَهُمُ الْكِتَٰبَ بِالْحَقِّ لِيَحْكُمَ بَيْنَ النَّاسِ فِيمَا اخْتَلَفُوا فِيهِ ۚ وَمَا اخْتَلَفَ فِيهِ إِلَّا الَّذِينَ أُوتُوهُ مِنۢ بَعْدِ مَا جَآءَتْهُمُ الْبَيِّنَٰتُ بَغْيًا بَيْنَهُمْ ۖ فَهَدَى اللَّهُ الَّذِينَ ءَامَنُوا لِمَا اخْتَلَفُوا فِيهِ مِنَ الْحَقِّ بِإِذْنِهِ ۗ وَاللَّهُ يَهْدِى مَن يَشَآءُ إِلَىٰ صِرَٰطٍ مُّسْتَقِيمٍ ۝

Mankind was [of] one religion [before their deviation]; then Allah sent the prophets as bringers of good tidings and warners and sent down with them the Scripture in truth to judge between the people concerning that in which they differed. And none differed over the Scripture except those who were given it - after the clear proofs came to them - out of jealous animosity among themselves. And Allah guided those who believed to the truth concerning that over which they had differed, by His permission. And Allah guides whom He wills to a straight path. [2:213]

Islamic quotes of Ibn al-Qayyim

(rahimahullah)

"The crying of the sinners is more loved to Allah than the tasbeeh of the arrogant."

"When you do not have knowledge someone can bring you dirt and you will believe it is gold."

"A persons' tongue can give you the taste of His heart."

"Patience is when the heart doesn't lament and the mouth doesn't complain." –

"If scholars are wicked and worshippers are ignorant, the trial will be severe." –

"There is nothing more beneficial to the heart than reciting the Quran."

"Many ignorant people rely upon Allah's mercy and forgiveness yet forget that He is also severe in punishment."

"A deprivation of a few moments [of pleasure] is better than permanent regret."

"Satisfaction is when a person submits himself to his Lord."

"Allah will never humiliate one who takes his Lord as a friend and protector."

"Indeed the Believer who has reliance upon Allah, if the creation plot against him, Allah plots for him on his behalf and brings about victory for him, without any effort or strength from himself."

"Who sincerely relies on Allah to achieve something, will achieve it."

"Misdeeds stand as a block for earning. Surely, one can be deprived of provision by committing sins."

"Knowledge is not about narrating a lot but it is about Taqwa (piety)."

"If you knew Allah as He should be known, you would leave people aside and take Him as your Companion."

"Allah is displeased when you stop asking him and mankind is displeased when asked."

"O you who are patient! Bear a little more, just a little more remains."

"If the human knew the pleasure of meeting Allah and being near to him, then he (human) would feel grief for being distant from him (Allah)."

"All hard work is easy for the believers when they understand that Allah hears them."

"Allah promised you the pleasures of the Hereafter, so do not be in a hurry and seek them in this worldly life as if you are cutting plants before their harvest time, while they are much better if you wait. Likewise, the pleasures of the Hereafter are so much better."

"Our life in this world is like that of a harvest field. What you plant here is what you will eat in the hereafter."

"Be to Allah as He wishes, and He will be to you more than you can wish for."

"Allah loves from his slave that he beautifies his tongue with the truth, and his heart with Ikhlaas and love, turning repentantly and reliance upon Allah."

"A sign of well-being and success is that when one increases in knowledge, he becomes more humble and merciful."

"It is a punishment for a sinner, indulging in sins, to eventually be forgotten by Allah and left alone with devil."

"The sincere person has humility for Allah alone and hope in him alone, requesting from him alone."

"The soul will never become pious and purified except through undergoing afflictions. It is the same as gold that can never be pure except after removing all the base metals in it."

"The people of Quran are those who read it and act upon it, even if they have not memorized it."

"Whoever wrongs you and then comes in order to apologize then you should accept his apology out of humbleness and leave his intention up to Allah, exalted is He."

"O people who take pleasure in a life that will disappear; falling in love with a fading shadow is pure stupidity."

"Knowledge is a carpet, none treads upon it except for the one near (to Allah)."

"Love is a spring well that does not dry up. Its purity and sweetness increases when it is for the sake of Allah and in the way of Allah."

"The best of those who fast are the ones who fast who are more plentiful in the (legislated) Dhikr (remembrance) of Allah, the mighty and majestic, during their fast."

"If Allah wills goodness for a slave, he would prevent him from feeling good about his deeds and from telling others about them, and would busy him with thinking about his sins, and he will continue to be like this until he enters Paradise."

"The sinner does not feel any remorse over his sins. That is because his heart is already dead."

"A real man is the one who fears the death of his heart, not his body."

"Whenever sins increase, loneliness/gloom intensifies."

"When Allah is with you, then all worries, grief and sadness disappear; no grief can remain when Allah is with the slave."

"Wasting time is worse than death, because death separates you from this world whereas wasting time separates you from Allah."

"And the servant; if he exchanges disobedience with obedience, Allah will exchange the punishment upon him with pardoning (him), and humiliation with honor."

"Whoever desires to purify his heart, then let him prefer Allah to his desires."

"Perhaps you might me asleep while the doors of heaven are knocking with tens of supplications for you, by a poor person you aided, or a sad person you cheered up or a distressed person you brought relief to. Therefore don't underestimate doing good at all."

"If Allah the exalted, forgave a woman who gave water to a thirsty dog, what would he do the one who gives water to the thirsty, food to the hungry and dress to those Muslims who don't have clothes."

"Your nafs is just like your enemy, once it finds you serious, it obeys you. If it finds weakness from you, It will take you as prisoner."

"Every type of knowledge and action which doesn't increase the strength of imaan and yaqeen has been corrupted."

"For the person who repents and becomes better after a sin, the sin is a mercy."

"Whoever thinks of the greatness of Allah will never be at ease in committing wrong actions."

"Sitting with the poor and less fortunate people removes the ego and pride from your heart." –

"It is enough of an honor for you that you are His(Allah's) worshipper, and it is sufficient glory for you that He(Allah) is your Lord."

"Whoever wants to purify his heart, must prefer Allah over and above his own desires."

"As long as you pray, you knock on the door of Allah. And whoever knocks at the door of Allah, He will open it for him."

"Sins destroy the heart the same way poison destroys the body."

"Sins need to be burnt, either with the pain of regret in this world, or with the fire of hell in the Hereafter!"

"In the heart there is a void that can only be filled by loving Allah."

"If Allah wants well for a slave, He strips away from his heart the ability to see his own good deeds and speaking about them with his tongue, and preoccupies him with seeing his own sin, and it continues to remain in front of his eyes until he enters jannah."

"The servant of Allah who seeks the pleasure of Allah never abandons tawbah (repentance)."

"The intelligent person does not cling to this material world."

"Allah is displeased when you stop asking of Him and mankind is displeased when asked."

"The lover of the world cannot get rid from three things –

1. Constant worry

2. Permanent discomfort

3. Relentless distress."

"And when the eye no longer cries out of fear of Allaah, know that this drought originates from the hardness of the heart."

"Know the value of what was lost, and cry like someone who knows the value of what has passed him by."

"If the heart becomes hardened – the eye becomes dry."

"Dhikr is a tree with fruits of awareness. The more frequent dhikr is made, the stronger the roots of a tree and more fruits on it."

"Sins generate more sins, and one leads to another, until they overpower a man and he finds it difficult to repent from that. As one of the earlier generation said: One of the punishments of bad deeds is more bad deeds, and one of the rewards of good deeds is more good deeds."

"Satisfaction is when a person submits himself to his Lord (Allah)."

"Sinning will leave you poor and regretful."

"Some people remain deprived of knowledge due to their poor ability to remain silent."

"Allah created both paradise and hellfire for the sinners. Hellfire is for the sinner who sinned but didn't ask Allah for forgiveness. But paradise is for the sinner who sinned but turned to Allah and asked for his forgiveness."

"Deeds without sincerity are like a traveler who carries in his water jug dirt. The carrying of its burden him and it brings no benefit."

"This Dunya(world) is just like shadow, If you try to catch it, you will never be able to do so. But if you turn your back towards it, it has no choice but to follow you."

"Corruption of character arises from putting the creation between yourself and Allah, and by putting your ego between yourself and his creation."

"Don't carry anxiety for the future because it is in the hands of Allah."

"If a heart becomes attached to anything other than Allah, Allah makes him dependent on what he is attached to. And he will be betrayed by it."

"Friday is the balance of the week, Ramadan is the valance of the year and hajj is the balance of the life."

"Falling in love is a disease and its cure is to marry the one you love."

"When you make du'a it is a sign that Allah loves you and has intended good for you."

"When Allah tests you, it is never intended to destroy you. When He removes something in your possession, it is only in order to empty your hands for an even greater gift."

"Know the value of what was lost, and cry like someone who knows the value of what has passed him by."

"Undoubtedly, one should never please people by displeasing Allah."

"The heart gets sick as the body does and its cure is in asking for forgiveness and protection. It also becomes rusty like a mirror does and it is polished by remembering Allah. The heart can also be naked like the body and can lose its dress and decoration, which is piety.And it can feel hunger and thirst like the body does, and its nourishment is knowledge, love, trust, and offering service to Allah."

Great Books

Search by **ISBN** to buy the correct book

Stories of the Prophets	ISBN: 9781643543888
The Story of the Holy Prophet	ISBN: 9781643544267
The Noble Quran (Arabic)	ISBN: 9781643543994
Koran (English: Easy to Read)	ISBN: 9781643540924
Life in al-Barzakh: Life after Death	ISBN: 9781643544144
The Heavenly Dispute	ISBN: 9781643544168
The Journey of the Strangers	ISBN: 9781643544175
Disciplining the Soul	ISBN: 9781643544151
Timeless Seeds of Advice	ISBN: 9781643544120
Diseases of the Hearts & Cures	ISBN 9781643544106
The Friends of Allah	ISBN: 9781643544236
The Path to Guidance	ISBN: 9781643544052
Miracles of the Prophet	ISBN: 9781643544038
Seerah of Prophet Muhammad	ISBN: 9781643543222
Book on Islam and Marriage	ISBN: 9781073877140
The Spiritual Cure	ISBN: 9781643544212
Great Women of Islam	ISBN: 9781643543758
Stories of the Koran	ISBN: 9781095900796
The Purification of the Soul	ISBN: 9781643541389
Al-Fawaid: Wise Sayings	ISBN: 9781727812718
The Book of Hajj	ISBN: 9781072243335
40 Hadith Qudsi	ISBN: 9781070655949
40 Hadith Nawawi	ISBN: 9781070547428
The Legacy of the Prophet	ISBN: 9781080249343

The Ideal Muslim Woman   ISBN: 9781643543192

The Soul's Journey after Death   ISBN: 9781643541365

Khalid Bin Al-Waleed   ISBN: 9781643543420

The Islamic View of Jesus   ISBN: 978164354335

Don't Be Sad   ISBN: 9781643543451

Ota Benga   ISBN: 9798698096665